Christopher Po

Enter the Circus

Bumblebee Books
London

BUMBLEBEE PAPERBACK EDITION

A CIP catalogue record for this title is
available from the British Library.

ISBN: 978-1-83934-068-0

Bumblebee Books is an imprint of
Olympia Publishers.

First Published in 2021

Bumblebee Books
Tallis House
2 Tallis Street
London
EC4Y 0AB

Printed in Great Britain

www.olympiapublishers.com

Dedication

To Rebecca:

If I could name a new star in the sky, I would call it Rebecca. Philosophers, poets, travellers and astronomers have all been inspired by stars just as you inspire me. You shine your light on my journey and guide me through the passing days like a bright beacon of hope.

To my mom and dad:

You gave me the gift of a happy childhood. You bought me books and you helped me read them. You took me to places that captured my mind and my heart. You gave me love each day and allowed me to flourish.

To Richard:

You were my brother and playmate. You helped me to indulge my imagination in our games and you were by my side as I grew to appreciate what a beautiful gift family is.

To my nan's, grandads, aunts and uncles:

You have been the frame around the world I have known. You've helped the picture stay bright and vibrant

To my teachers:

You nurtured my knowledge and gave encouragement for me to thirst for more.

To the poets:

You have the truest hearts. Your passions and hopes and your fears and delights have captured me so many times and will forever continue to do so.

To Mr Kam Balaggan and Mr Don Williams:

Thank you so much for your kindness, expertise and for saving my eyesight. I could not have asked for two better people looking after my care and recovery.

Contents

Introduction

It was December and Clarence yawned peacefully as he curled up in front of the fire. Sleep was his favourite thing in the world and as the snow tumbled tranquilly outside of the window, Clarence's eyes became heavy.

THUD!

Scamper came hurtling in, bouncing all over Clarence's head and clambering all over his back!

"Time to play!" he woofed happily.

"I'm old!" snapped Clarence, "I don't play anymore! I just want to sleep! There are better things to do than waste all your energy bouncing about! Now leave me be!"

"You're never too old to play!" cried Scamper.

"If you can show me a game where I don't have to lift a single paw, or move a single hair on my body, I will play with you," declared Clarence, feeling quite confident that this would prove an impossible task for his young friend.

"Look into the fire," Scamper ordered triumphantly, "what do you see?"

"Flames!" snapped Clarence impatiently.

"Look harder!"

"Coal... ash... smoke!"

"Can't you see the dragon clawing at the castle walls?" asked Scamper. "What about the eagle rising up from behind the mountain and spreading its great wings?"

Clarence squinted his eyes. The flames began to take on

new shapes, the colours became more intense and no longer did the grate hold a fire but a theatre of the magical and the unexpected. Soon he was glimpsing wizards hunched over cauldrons; hearing the crack of the whip as the lion tamer attempted to subdue the roar of the jungle king; and spying mysterious shadows from other realms tower and shrink in the hazy distance. The rhythm and warmth of the hypnotic blaze had soon sent Clarence into the deepest of sleeps.

Scamper too, despite his unquenchable zeal and energy, had sunk into a peaceful slumber. Curled up, side by side, they dozed as the world outside was painted the most glorious white by Winter herself. As she passed through the garden, Winter momentarily looked through the window and saw the two companions. She smiled, placed a small object outside the front door and then went on her way as Winter often does.

Months passed and it was decided that Scamper was moving to a new house.

"Bye then!" said Scamper, "I'm off to see the world! I will miss you." He gave Clarence a lick and bounded off out of the door. "At least you will get your sleep now!" he called back teasingly.

But Clarence no longer wanted to sleep. What was sleep without Scamper to wake him up? He stared into the cold and empty fireplace and sighed. In that moment, he realised how precious his time was, how all those moments he wanted to doze were moments he had wasted. Age had faded him. Scamper made him young. He gave a lonely howl and slumped down onto his rug.

THUD!

Clarence shot up with a start! Something had jumped on his head!

"I knew you loved me really!" came a laugh.

It was Scamper! He was back!

"I've brought you something that I found! It's something amazing and special—an unmelted snowflake!" Scamper nudged it towards Clarence and in that instant, the sky grew darker, the temperature dropped, and the fire sprang to life!

"A little piece of winter," marvelled Clarence.

"Fancy a game?" asked Scamper.

Within minutes, they were both dreaming up the mysterious things that lay before them in the world of scarlet, orange and yellow. Through Scamper's eyes, Clarence's world was brought back to life.

Imagination and sharing has a tendency to do that. It doesn't matter if you're a dog or a person.

Though it was now the reign of Spring, from another place and time, Winter looked on and smiled once again.

It was quite the gift she had left behind.

This book is not a gift of snowflakes but a gift of words. I hope it lights up your days and lingers through your lives like a flame which never fades.

On a Night in Chamberlain Square

When the clouds are a blanket,
Which wrap up the moon,
And the hour is as dark,
As a heart without love,
And the stars have grown dim,
Like a tarnished old spoon,
And their glow does not shine,
From the sky up above,
When the policeman grows sleepy,
As the miles of his beat,
Cause him to pause,
In Chamberlain Square,
And lean on the lamppost,
To rest his sore feet,
In the shadows, I'll linger,
Like smoke in the air.

When the wind has been raging,
Like a wolf on the prowl,
And garden gates rattle,
Like snakes on the roam,
When there's no one to see,
Save the ancient old owl,
For all are curled up,
In the warmth of their home,

When midnight is murky,
Like fog on the moor,
And sleep has long settled,
Each crack and each crag,
Like light through a window,
And ghosts through the door,
So swift do I move,
As I pilfer the swag.

When thoughts are elsewhere,
In a land of sweet dreams,
And the dawn is a promise,
Yet to fulfil,
With a sack full of loot,
And a heart full of schemes,
I creep like the frost,
In Novembertime's chill,
Whilst the policeman is thinking,
Of bacon and bread,
Of sausage and breakfast,
At break of the day,
I depart like the breath,
That escapes from the dead,
Up over the hills,
And then far away.

Snowy

Snowy was brilliant white,
Like fresh-poured milk,
The moon in the morning,
And seagull's wings in the glare of the sun.
Over walls, across the sands,
Through the woods,
We'd run and run.

When I was in the saddle,
I'd be a prince or highwayman,
A buccaneering pirate,
Every day, a different deed,
I was the adventurer,
And he, my noble steed.

Truest, truest friendship,
Where hours pass in minutes,
And the golden afternoon,
Melts into a twilight sky,
I would grow quite sleepy then,
But Snowy would watch over me,
With his steadfast countenance,
And black, unblinking eye.

On waking, he'd be ready,
Dutiful, obedient,
Unquestioning, he'd follow me,
Along my playful course,
The magic of a little boy,
Upon his wooden horse.

The Llama

A llama feels calmer,
When it's standing in a puddle,
But it flusters when in clusters,
With a camel in the middle,
For the camel's not a mammal,
That the llama likes to cuddle,
'Tis a loner is the llama,
And it's really not a riddle,
That it's jumpy and it's grumpy,
And it's woe-filled,
And it's wary,
When its idyll is polluted,
By a humpy,
Dromedary.

The Seagull Poem

Oh to be a seagull!
And poo on people's heads,
As they walk along the promenade,
Or tend their flower beds,
How lovely it would be,
To soar up in the sky,
To see folk just gaze up at you,
And hit them in the eye.

Yes, I wish I was a seagull,
I'd have a target list,
The people who annoyed me,
Because they just exist,
I'd squawk for their attention,
"Hey there! Down below!"
They'd glance towards the fluffy clouds,
And then I'd just let go.

I'd get the right consistency,
I'd eat things that I shouldn't
They might think they'd escape me,
But I guarantee, they wouldn't,
For my stomach would be rumbly,
And all churned up inside,
And when I'd get the urge to plop,
There's no place they could hide.

I'd search for them all over,
West, north, east and south,
I'd mess up all their hairdos,
And I'd get some in their mouth,
They'd shriek at me in terror,
They'd quake with helpless fear,
But their begging wouldn't save them,
From my seagull diarrhoea.

So watch out all humanity,
You'd best vacate this town,
For if you've vexed me bad today,
A nightmare's coming down!

My Kingdom for a Cup of Tea

The crown was sat upon the king,
Who sat upon his throne,
Lamenting that his servant folk,
Had left him on his own,
"I'll have to do things for myself."
Is all that he would groan.

"Now doing things is much too much,
For royalty like me,
The thought of work upon my mind,
Amounts to agony,
I would trade my wealthy kingdom,
For a lovely cup of tea."

Now traipsing through the cobbled streets,
A jester heard his cry,
"My kingdom for a cup of tea."
Is all the king would sigh,
The jester thought, 'What blissful luck!
I cannot pass this by.'

"I'll have a kingdom for myself,
I'll soon be in fine fettle."
The jester rubbed his sweaty palms,
His nerves just wouldn't settle,
Thus he promptly grabbed a teapot,
And began to boil the kettle.

Soon up the castle stairs he dashed,
Across the Persian rug,
"A cup of tea, your majesty!"
The jester felt so smug,
As he bowed before the thirsty king,
And handed him a mug.

"At last!" The king said gratefully,
"A brew to whet my throat."
"It's the best tea you will ever have,"
The jester gave a gloat,
"The teabags are the finest,
Though, the water's from the moat."

Now once the king had drunk his fill,
The jester said, "I think,
You may regret a small amount,
Indulging in that drink,
But as the mug is empty,
You should wash it in the sink."

"How dare you!" cried the angry king,
"To order me about –
To show such sheer impertinence,
Will cost you, I've no doubt,
For now I will imprison you,
And never let you out."

The jester laughed, "You silly man,
I'll order who I will.
I made for you a cup of tea,
Now you must pay the bill –
Your precious kingdom is the cost."
(The king now looked quite ill!)

"You've tricked me!" sobbed the sorry king,
(Who was the king no more)
"Well, that's tough luck," the jester grinned,
"I think you know the score,
You're standing in my castle,
Would you show yourself the door?"

And so the king, (who now was not)
Emerged out of the foyer,
And as sure as raindrops taste like snow,
Or beans are made from soya,
He said, "I am a victim now,
I'll find myself a lawyer."

Now that's exactly what he did,
The lawyer said, "Oh dear!
You've made a very bad mistake,
But you need not have fear –
I'll get you off the so-called hook –
I'll see you in the clear."

"Oh thank you!" cried the former king,
(Who we shall now call K,
On account his rule was in the past,
And that was far away,
Thus to call him king would be a lie,
What more is there to say?)

Well actually, there is more left,
For K in jubilation,
Told the lawyer he would hold,
A splendid celebration,
If he helped him get his kingdom back,
Through witty inspiration.

"A celebration's not enough,"
The lawyer promptly said.
"My costs exceed a mere feast,
As I must use my head,
You'll have to think of something else,
To pay me with instead!"

“I’ll tell you what,” said K, with haste,
“If you get me restored,
I will give you anything you want,
Now are we in accord?
When I’m back upon the throne,
You pick your own reward.”

Now as both men had struck the deal,
The issue went to court.
The jester (now the new king) said,
“I really think you ought,
Be thankful that I’m here at all –
I’m such a splendid sport!”

And hence the lawyer took the stand,
And thus commenced the trial.
“The first witness that I call is K,
Now this may take a while…
To begin with you requested tea,
I’m sure you’ve no denial?”

The question asked, no answer came,
The lawyer gave a cough,
The judge was bored, the jury laughed,
The jester gave a scoff,
The clerk thought he should quickly wake,
Poor K (who had dozed off!)

"G," said K, "I've missed my Q,
U C Y this could B?
I find it hard to now XL,
(I am an OAP)
I was labelled HRH U know,
Until I asked for T.
To be complete I'll add FM,
And Z and S and D
I think I've used all letters now,
Pray, have I missed NE?"

"Indeed you have," the jester spoke,
For example J and V,
And not forgetting W."
Said K, "That's only three!
I'd shorten the whole alphabet,
If it were down to me."

"I do object!" the judge implored,
"The question does remain,
You swapped your kingdom for some tea?"
Said K, "I was insane,
Or at very least, my massive thirst,
Impeded use of brain!"

"It's no matter," said the lawyer,
"For the case, it ends right now."
And pointing to the jester king,
(To whom he did not bow)
"I'll strip this fool of majesty,
And shall I tell you how?

The old king craved a cup of tea,
And in time, he took his sup.
Then in exchange, the old king's crown,
Was swiftly given up,
Yet the jester utilized a MUG -
A MUG is not a CUP!"

"Magnificent!" remarked the judge –
"The prosecution's won,
The jester king has no defence,
And thus his reign is done,
The crown must now be given back –
Now isn't this such fun?"

Traumatised, the jester wept,
"I'm back to being a clown!"
Triumphantly, old K rejoiced,
"I'm back – I have my crown,
(Thus, now we'll call him King again,
For such is his renown!)

Now this was very well and good,
But things then went amiss,
For the lawyer said, "I hate to spoil,
The kingdom's newfound bliss,
But now I want my recompense,
Now let me reminisce…

You said I could have anything,
And I've had time to muse,
I think I'll have your kingdom please,
Yes, that is what I choose."
The judge then turned and told the king,
"The kingdom's gone - you lose!"

The greedy lawyer took the lot,
Castle, crown and reign –
The jester got off lightly,
Though, some say he suffered pain,
At knowing that he'd been the king,
Yet wouldn't be again.

And the king who was initially,
Subsequently, but not since,
At some point in the meantime,
Whilst dining on some quince,
Ruefully remembered,
His blunder with a wince.

"There are many lessons in this life,
And so, I must suppose,
There's been a lesson here as well -
I don't know how it goes –
I'd give my life to anyone,
Who really, truly knows..."

He was lucky no one heard him,
For life is very prized,
And yet he'd promised it away,
And never realised,
Do you think if someone claimed it,
He'd have been a tad surprised?

The chances are, I bet he would,
And thus it's for the best,
That if you're like that lazy king,
And all you crave is rest,
You now pay close attention
Of this rather small request:

Don't promise things that you quite like,
When you don't want to do,
A boring task like making tea,
Or problems may ensue,
Promise things you don't like much,
And this may get you through.

For example, an old cardigan,
Socks or underwear,
For if you have to give them up,
It is something you could bear,
And that's better for emotion,
(As you simply would not care!)

But if you really love all things,
Like crowns and thrones and health,
If you think your underwear's,
A mainstay of your wealth -
You need not promise anything,
Just do things for yourself!

Porky

I had a pig called Porky,
I loved him very much,
Though he wasn't very talky,
He was nice to pat and touch.
He lived with me upon our farm,
Until one cloudy day,
Porky wasn't there no more,
Porky went away.

Now Porky was my closest friend,
Without him, it was sad,
"Don't worry son," my father said,
"Life isn't all that bad –
I know that you are missing him,
I know you're feeling down,
So I've brought you home a special treat,
From when I went to town."

Now sausages I really loved,
And that's what Dad brought back,
But he hadn't just brought five or six,
He seemed to have a stack.
"I know they can't replace him son,
But I hope that you will find,
These yummy scummy sausages,
Take Porky off your mind."

I could see he'd made an effort,
So I tried to act more cheery,
"Where does sausage come from Dad?"
No answer – "Did you hear me?"
"Ermm yes son, and the answer is,
The answer… let me think…
Would you like another sausage son?
Here, have an extra link."

"I'll have another if you like,
Now what about my question?"
"I'm afraid I'm not that sure son,
Besides, I've indigestion –
Perhaps you have another thing,
That I can ponder on?"
"I have – a most important thing –
Where has Porky gone?"

"He may have gone on holiday,
He might be at the zoo,
Would you like another sausage son?
I haven't got a clue."
"Don't worry Dad, it's quite okay,
It's really strange somehow,
I almost get the feeling,
That Porky's with us now."

Dad said, "That's the spirit son,
It's good to think like that,
Porky was a good pig,
Nice and round and fat.
He'll always be inside of you,
For he was just so swell,
Yes, Porky was a good pig,
He really went down well!"

Of Foolishness with Fritters

Freddy Finger, feeling fatter,
Thought it finer feeling fitter,
Feeling fitter he felt finer,
For a treat he fried a fritter,
Frying fritters made him fatter,
So, he made the batter thinner,
Thinner batter didn't matter,
Freddy's tummy got no flatter.

Freddy Finger, feeling flustered,
Thought it foolish that he'd faltered,
Faltering, his arms a-flailing,
Fuming Freddy feebly failing,
Feebly failing frying fritters,
Fritter frying sadly foiling,
Freddy's belly's flubber flowing,
Thinness fading, fatness growing.

Freddy Fritter frying fingers,
Sorry… Finger frying fritters,
Fatty fritters, Freddy feeling,
Thinness flagging, too much feeding,
Flippant Freddy, thus frustrated,
Frankly said it was fictitious,
Feeling fine was overrated,
Frying fritters too delicious.

The Princess and the Pirate

Of all the pirates in the world to have sailed the seven seas,
The most feared was Cutthroat Joe,
He was brash, he was mean, he was sadly obscene,
And the worst of the worst of foe.
He downed eleven bottles of whisky a day,
And several barrels of rum,
With all this drink he could not think,
So, his mind was awfully numb.

Now the thing with Cutthroat Joe, was the fact he never washed,
His hygiene had gone down the drain, thanks to him being sloshed,
No ship would near his vessel, for the truth to you I'll tell,
The fragrance in the air made every sailor feel unwell,
Then in a few quick seconds, they'd collapse upon the spot,
And all their hidden treasures, Cutthroat Joe would steal the lot.

This pirate sailed the ocean blue,
Head of a one-man gang,
Wherever he went, he left his scent,
And this is what he sang:

"My name is Cutthroat Joe, and I smell just like a sewer,
My armpits reek like stale milk, and my breath is like manure,
My gums are all decayed, and my teeth are hanging out –
But I sing my song, as I like my pong –
It's great just being a lout!"

Now in the town on Seaweed Bay, the people knew too well,
That Cutthroat Joe would soon return - armed with putrid smell,
He'd raid the coast, and steal their gold, then sail back out to sea,
"We need a hero!" cried the Mayor, "This simply cannot be."
But no one in the country volunteered to catch the slob,
Until the Princess of the kingdom said that she would do the job.

"Preposterous!" declared the King, "Outrageous!" cried the Queen,
"He is such a filthy man, and you are so serene."
"You're just a girl!" remarked the Earl, "You've not the strength to cope,
With his vast array of odours - you haven't got a hope."
But the Princess did not heed these words,
And armed with peg on nose,
She sailed out to Cutthroat's ship –
The famous 'Wilted Rose'.

She climbed the deck determined, to prove her family wrong,
And for the confrontation, she would not be waiting long,
For standing there the pirate, he looked so big and strong,
And on seeing her he chuckled and blurted out his song:
"My name is Cutthroat Joe, and my socks have all gone musty,
There is mould beneath my toenails, and my skin has all gone crusty,
I eat the lice within my beard and the maggots from my flesh,
Plus, there's nothing like a bogey when it's nice and warm and fresh,
And now you'll be my hostage, where you'll squeeze my spots by day,
So, your spirits will be broken, as you'll never get away."

Now the Princess was not worried, she had a glow in both her eyes,
As she handed Joe a lozenge of near colossus size,
"Suck this sweet my fierce friend – you'll get a nice surprise!"
Then as he sucked, his nose unblocked, and there he fell and died.

The Princess smiled with utmost glee, and headed for the coast,
And when asked of what she'd done, she couldn't help but boast,
"My loving King, my gracious Queen, there's nothing much to tell –
I knew he would not be alive, if he'd a sense of smell,
So, I thought I'd clear his airways, and when his nostrils chanced to flare,
He went all stiff and smelled a whiff he simply could not bear."

So Seaweed Bay rejoiced, free from threats of plunder –
All because old Cutthroat had made a dreadful blunder,
But the 'Wilted Rose' still drifts, abandoned and alone,
And on her deck there seems to be an 'eerie' sort of moan -
The ghost of a drunken pirate, against the silvery moon,
Lamenting on his last mistake, he sings his final tune:

"My name was Cutthroat Joe, and I stank just like a rat,
I sucked a sweet and sniffed my feet,
And couldn't handle that.
So now I am no more, but I've learnt a lesson since,
When you sweat,
Do not forget,
To have a proper rinse!"

The Changing Moon

Up in the sky,
The moon is full,
A great big ball,
Of cotton wool,

Looking down,
I watch her peer,
A ball of snow,
A shining sphere,

But other days,
She seems much thinner,
Like she's gone without
Her dinner,

I call out loud,
Toward the crescent,
"You're paler now,
Less effervescent."

Then later on,
I might infer,
That maybe,
I've offended her,

She started big,
And changed to small,
And now she isn't there,
At all!

And so I wonder,
If or when,
She'll one day,
Venture back again.

Unblinking Eyes

I stand beneath the distant stars,
That gaze with their unblinking eyes,
And wonder if they notice me,
From where they hang up in the skies.

For now, tonight, I look to them,
With heart of hope and head of dreams,
And flowing thoughts that seek a path,
Like rivers that start out as streams.

For I've been a sailor lost at sea,
I've been a painter robbed of light,
I've been a poet stripped of words,
And all amid a cloudy night.

To be a sculptor without stone,
Or a thinker with an empty mind,
Is to be an actor on the stage,
Who, impassive, just reads out the lines.

To rob a script of all its heart,
To let all colour fade to grey,
To have a frame that holds no art,
Is to take the meaning from each day.

So I stand beneath those distant stars,
That gaze from heaven, up above,
And my soul, at last, re-finds itself,
And fills with peace,
And faith
And love.

Pog the Wizard

Want a rabbit?
Watch me grab it,
Out my purple hat!
Good gosh! Be praised!
The crowd amazed,
Now would you fancy that?
Poggilly ogilly,
Poggilly ogilly,
Poggilly ogilly ooooh,
Duck Face! Duck Face!
Duck Face!
Duck Face!
Watch what I can do!

Please don't thank me!
Got a hankie?
Watch it disappear!
Brightest blue,
In front of you,
And then, it's out of here!
Poggilly ogilly,
Poggilly ogilly,
Poggilly ogilly ooooh,
Duck Face! Duck Face!
Duck Face!
Duck Face!
Watch what I can do!

Now here's a thing!
A golden ring!
Sat there on your finger!
You have it on,
Not now – it's gone,
These gold rings do not linger!
Poggilly ogilly,
Poggilly ogilly,
Poggilly ogilly ooooh,
Duck Face! Duck Face!
Duck Face!
Duck Face!
Watch what I can do!

A paper sheet –
It's quite complete,
I rip it up and then,
I cast a spell,
And all is well,
The sheet's complete again!
Poggilly ogilly,
Poggilly ogilly,
Poggilly ogilly ooooh,
Duck Face! Duck Face!
Duck Face!
Duck Face!
Watch what I can do!

My final trick
Is nice and slick,
A hazy cloud of smoke,

Once it's cleared,
I've disappeared -
It really is no joke!
Poggilly ogilly,
Poggilly ogilly,
Poggilly ogilly ooooh,
Duck Face! Duck Face!
Duck Face!
Duck Face!
Watch what I can do!

Where I go,
You do not know,
For I have left the scene,
Out of reach,
A far-off beach,
Eating jam and cream!
Poggilly ogilly,
Poggilly ogilly,
Poggilly ogilly ooooh,
Duck Face! Duck Face!
Duck Face!
Duck Face!
Watch what I can do!

The Knight and the Dragon

'HELP US!'
Read the sign -
'DRAGON NEEDS A-SLAYING,
THE KING, HE HAS A FORTUNE,
(And he's very happy paying)
Think of the ACKNOWLEDGEMENT,
HIP-HIP HOORAY, WOO-HOO!
(Apply within the castle)
(Any fool will do)'

"Easy!"
Said the knight,
(Who was gluttonous and greedy)
"I am strong and brave,
And the kingdom's gone all needy.
I'll do it!" he said proudly,
"Please trust me; I'm your man,
I'd do anything for payment,
Though I haven't got a plan!"

"Accepted!"
Said the servant,
(Who worked within the castle)
"You needn't fill in any forms,
It isn't worth the hassle.

Best of luck and off you go,
Please take this sword and horse -
Yours to keep, so cheerio,
And may you stay the course."

"Greetings!"
Said the knight,
As he reached the dragon's lair,
"I'm afraid I've come to slay you –
Are you happy? Is it fair?
Well, it doesn't really matter,
I have not come here to fail –
There's a bounty on your head,
Which I'll get if I prevail."

"Mmmm – tasty!"
Sighed the dragon,
As he gobbled down the knight,
"The armour was quite crunchy,
But the skin was roasted right,
Yet, I do think it's a pity,
When these heroes come to dazzle,
Arriving, chasing glory,
And I fry them to a frazzle!"

'HE'S DEAD!'
Read the obituary,
'The chance he stood was slim,
He tried to be a legend,
But it wasn't meant for him.
It's very, very sad,
The fact that he is gone,
But true to knightly fashion,
We'll accept it and move on!'

'PLEASE HELP US!'
Read the sign –
'Dragon's getting frisky,
We're sure it is achievable,
And isn't very risky!
We will bill you as a Lancelot –
With superstardom rating!'
But no one has applied since,
And the dragon is still waiting...

Tulip Tides

Tulips are a sea of red,
Cascading in the month of May,
So vibrant in their soil bed,
To brighten up the day.

I swim within their pretty scent,
And know how glad I am,
To have a passing hour spent,
With thoughts of Amsterdam.

And in the winter months ahead,
I'll plant their bulbs once more,
And in spring, I'll see my scarlet tide,
Against my grassy shore.

On Behalf of All Pigs

There are so many creatures, with interesting features,
The camel has humps, one or two,
The elephant's trunk and the smell of the skunk,
Or the pouch found on each kangaroo,
But is it not rotten, that pigs are forgotten,
And called lazy and sloppy and fat?
Please have a heart, as I proudly impart,
That pigs are much more than that.

Snakes have a slither, which cause you to quiver,
Spiders go bump in the night,
A scorpion's tail can force you to wail,
And lizards can give you a fright,
But a pig cannot harm from its home on the farm,
Where we gobble our food from the trough,
Yet our bellies will spark some hurtful remarks,
From people who tease us and scoff.

Giraffes can stand proud, with their heads in the clouds,
Lions parade with their crown,
Nobody snipes at a tiger with stripes,
Or runs a buffalo down,
Yet pigs are called bland and fail to command,
The respect that we think we are due,
We may be quite round, but our outlook is sound,
So, we seek some kindness from you.

Not many are neater than quick-legged cheetahs,
Or wiser than brainy old owls,
A gibbon will preen to keep itself clean,
As will cockerels and fowls,
Yet we pigs are the studs who bath in the mud,
To keep our complexions divine,
We really get shirty when folk call us dirty,
Such comments are way out of line.

Dolphins are charming, whilst sharks are alarming,
The rhino's incredibly cross,
Now you're all too aware when a grizzly bear,
Intends to show he's the boss.
But for your attention, we'd just like to mention,
That pigs are inherently great:
In life we are winners, and what's more on your dinners,
We taste just as good on your plate!

Wrong′uns

Andrew Richards threw the rubber sir –
I clean on saw him do it!
Sarah Porter got a piece of gum –
I heard her start to chew it!
Daniel Rigsby took the hamster cage,
Then set the hamster free,
All of them are wrong′uns sir,
But I'm not sir, not me!

Eve Murphy flashed her fake tattoo,
Now sir, they're not allowed,
Then Georgia Dunn, she stole my bun,
And lobbed it at a crowd,
Kris Jennings bobbed his tongue out sir,
T'was as red as red could be,
All of them are wrong′uns sir,
But I'm not sir, not me!

Dave Kitson's got a stink bomb sir,
He's left it in the loo,
I think it's on a timer sir,
And set for five-past-two,
And sir, you know Steph Atkinson,
She took your secret key –
All of them are wrong′uns sir,
But I'm not sir, not me!

Miss Hargreaves's kissing parents sir,
Miss Aktar's skirt's too short,
Mr Pickford swore in lessons sir,
He should be on report,
Mrs Dawson's cuffed a student sir,
He made an awful fuss,
Yes, all of them are wrong'uns sir,
But we're not sir, not us!

To the Boats

To the boats we go,
And the old wooden pier,
Some to set sail,
And some just to stare,
Watch as they row,
On waters so clear,
As in peace they inhale,
The summertime air.

The mountain's a frame,
At the edge of the lake,
Green, gold and brown,
At the chiming of noon;
Gliding on water,
The swan and the drake,
Chasing the spot,
Where the breadcrumbs are strewn.

Picnics on grass,
With a tablecloth mat,
Checked red and white,
'Neath a blanket of sky,
A sandwich of jam,
And a lemonade glass,
And the taste of cake,
Or a sweet apple pie.

To the sweeping of oars,
We close up our eyes,
Drift somewhere else,
As minutes will run,
Lose track of time,
For there’s no place to be,
In this trance of July,
In the kiss of the sun.

The Safari Park

Down in the safari park, Grandad needs a wee,
The lion is a-roaming and the leopard's up a tree,
The hyenas are a-prowling and the tiger's in the wood,
And all of them...
Yes all of them,
Think Grandad's looking good.

"I have to go," said Grandad with a 'cannot hold it' frown,
"You'll have to wait," said Father, "for the car has broken down."
"But my bladder's not as strong as yours – I'm very, very old!"
"Grandad you must listen...
Stop a bit and listen,
You must do as you are told!"

Down in the safari park, Grandad's going red,
There's a crocodile behind us and a polar bear ahead,
There's a python and a cougar and a jaguar with claws,
Lots of hungry animals...
So many hungry animals...
A host of hungry animals,
Alert with open jaws.

"I'm fit to burst," said Grandad, "I must leg it to the loo,
It's only ninety yards away, what else is there to do?"
"But Grandad you won't make it, your legs are worn and stiff!"
"Nonsense!" shouted Grandad,
"Piffle!" shouted Grandad,
"Ridiculous!" cried Grandad –
"I could get there in a jiff!"

Down in the safari park, we need a gun to shoot!
There's a gator on the bonnet and a boa in the boot,
There's a cheetah on the sunroof with a grumble in her tummy,
All of them eye Grandad...
Greedily eye Grandad,
Longingly eye Grandad,
For they think he's looking yummy.

But suddenly, inside the car, Grandad's gone all quiet,
No longer is he wriggling and acting all defiant,
"I think I'm safe," he whispered – "I could not take the chance,
I tried my best to hold it...
I tried so hard to hold it,
But I found I couldn't hold it,
So I did it in my pants!"

In Amongst the Roses

Rebecca thought it better,
With her roses smelling sweeter,
She thrust her head amongst them,
And it made her feel completer,
Nectar was perfecta,
To her finest tuned of noses,
As she thrived and came alive,
With her face within her roses.

This hobby (in the lobby)
Of her gorgeous Tudor castle,
Was joyous at the start of things,
But soon became a hassle:
In patches, she got scratches,
So, her mood became quite darkish,
Thorns have that effect on things –
They're pointy and quite sharpish!

Snug

I am snug,
As a bug,
In a rug,
Tonight,
The world is outside,
And I am wrapped tight,
With my blanket around me,
To keep off the dark,
I hear the rain patter,
I hear the dogs bark,
And the wind, like a river,
As it surges through trees,
But my blanket protects me,
On nights such as these.

The storm may be howling,
The sea may be churning,
The tempest is bubbling,
Boiling and burning,
With the thud of the thunder,
And waves upon rocks,
And the creaking of ships,
As they groan in the docks,
Yes, it's all of a flurry,
Of that, there's no doubt,
But with my blanket around me,
All of that is kept out.

So, contentedly I smile,
As I hunker in my bed,
I could be out of doors tonight,
But I am here instead,
Watching as the lightning bolts,
Cascade amid the crashes,
The shadows of a moonless night,
Appear in vibrant flashes,
And for the briefest instant,
Amid the gusty squall,
Silhouettes are dancing,
Upon my bedroom wall.

But I am sound and snug tonight,
As the harbour clock strikes one,
I close my eyes...
Drift off to sleep...
Whilst life outside goes on.

I’d Offer You

I’d offer you the world,
If I thought that you would take it,
I’d offer you my heart,
If I thought you wouldn’t break it,
I’d offer you my smile,
If I thought you would reflect it,
I’d offer you my hand,
If I thought that you’d collect it,
I’d offer you my future,
If I thought that you would share it,
I’d offer you my soul,
If I thought you wouldn’t tear it,
I’d offer you my everything,
For how I think we’d glisten,
But if I found the strength to speak,
I wonder,
Would you listen?

Beefy

I had a cow called Beefy,
He was a treasured friend,
I thought we'd be together,
From the start until the end,
And although I still missed Porky,
(That's my pig, if you've forgot)
Beefy was a comfort,
He really helped a lot.

For many months, things were fine,
But then it all went wrong.
One morning Beefy wasn't there,
I thought that we were strong,
"Dad," I cried, "Beefy's left –
He always seemed so happy."
"Don't cry!" said Dad, "Don't feel bereft,
Now there's a gallant chappy.

Crying makes you hungry son,
How about a little snack?
I've just brought in some beef burgers,
I'll grill them on the rack,
Beefy wouldn't want you starving son,
He'd want to see you fed –
Try and think of something else,
Get Beefy out your head."

Now Dad was really trying,
So I took a calming breath,
"Where do burgers come from Dad?"
No answer – "Are you deaf?"
"No, my son, I heard you well,
I heard you loud and clear,
Burgers come from Timbuktu,
And places far from here."

"No burgers come from England Dad?"
"No… we lack the means,
We only have the weather for,
Sprouts and runner beans,
Anything else you want to ask?"
"Where did Beefy go?"
"That's very hard to answer son,
That's hard for me to know.

He could be at a ski resort,
He could be on the beach,
I know it's traumatised you son,
That Beefy's out of reach."
"Oh Dad! If only Beefy stayed,
He'd now be safe from harm,
For the safest place for animals,
Is here upon our farm."

Dad said, “That’s exactly right,
The farm is full of joy,
Beefy was a good cow,
And you’re a goodly boy,
I’m sure he will remember you,
It is a hurtful waste,
But likewise, we’ll remember him –
A cow of splendid taste!”

Exploring in the Garden

Exploring in the garden, this is what I found:
A teeny baby worm, which was peeking out the ground.

Exploring in the garden, this is what I found:
A snail with a shell that was big and brown and round,
And a teeny baby worm which was peeking out the ground.

Exploring in the garden, this is what I found:
A bumblebee up in the tree,
A wasp which had it in for me,
A snail with a shell that was big and brown and round,
And a teeny baby worm which was peeking out the ground.

Exploring in the garden, this is what I found:
A butterfly that fluttered by,
A very moody dragonfly,
A bumblebee up in the tree,
A wasp which had it in for me,
A snail with a shell that was big and brown and round,
And a teeny baby worm which was peeking out the ground.

Exploring in the garden, this is what I found:
A spider spinning on a log,
A warty toad,
A slimy frog,

A butterfly that fluttered by,
A very moody dragonfly,
A bumblebee up in the tree,
A wasp which had it in for me,
A snail with a shell that was big and brown and round,
And a teeny baby worm which was peeking out the ground.

Exploring in the garden, this is what I found:
A ladybird with seven spots,
A beetle hiding in some pots,
A spider spinning on a log,
A warty toad,
A slimy frog,
A butterfly that fluttered by,
A very moody dragonfly,
A bumblebee up in the tree,
A wasp which had it in for me,
A snail with a shell that was big and brown and round,
And a teeny baby worm which was peeking out the ground.

Exploring in the garden, this is what I found:
A hedgehog sleeping snug at rest,
A busy bird that built a nest,
A ladybird with seven spots,
A beetle hiding in some pots,
A spider spinning on a log,
A warty toad,
A slimy frog,
A butterfly that fluttered by,
A very moody dragonfly,
A bumblebee up in the tree,

A wasp which had it in for me,
A snail with a shell that was big and brown and round,
And a teeny baby worm which was peeking out the ground.

Exploring in the garden, this is what I found:
A caterpillar on a leaf,
A bench that had a mouse beneath,
A hedgehog sleeping snug at rest,
A busy bird that built a nest,
A ladybird with seven spots,
A beetle hiding in some pots,
A spider spinning on a log,
A warty toad,
A slimy frog,
A butterfly that fluttered by,
A very moody dragonfly,
A bumblebee up in the tree,
A wasp which had it in for me,
A snail with a shell that was big and brown and round,
And a teeny baby worm which was peeking out the ground.

Exploring in the garden, this is what I found:
A cat a-sneaking on the wall,
A hungry dog who hoped he'd fall,
A caterpillar on a leaf,
A bench that had a mouse beneath,
A hedgehog sleeping snug at rest,
A busy bird that built a nest,
A ladybird with seven spots,
A beetle hiding in some pots,
A spider spinning on a log,

A warty toad,
A slimy frog,
A butterfly that fluttered by,
A very moody dragonfly,
A bumblebee up in the tree,
A wasp which had it in for me,
A snail with a shell that was big and brown and round,
And a teeny baby worm which was peeking out the ground.

Exploring in the garden, this is what I found:
My mom who said, "It's time for tea –
You've seen all things there are to see!"
A cat a-sneaking on the wall,
A hungry dog who hoped he'd fall,
A caterpillar on a leaf,
A bench that had a mouse beneath,
A hedgehog sleeping snug at rest,
A busy bird that built a nest,
A ladybird with seven spots,
A beetle hiding in some pots,
A spider spinning on a log,
A warty toad,
A slimy frog,
A butterfly that fluttered by,
A very moody dragonfly,
A bumblebee up in the tree,
A wasp which had it in for me,
A snail with a shell that was big and brown and round,
And a teeny baby worm which was peeking out the ground.

Thoughts on a Poet

A poet is a potter,
Takes words,
Spins them on a wheel,
Crafts them and shapes them,
Makes their meaning real,

A poet is a conjurer,
Sprinkles magic,
Lets imagination fly,
Grows dreams from out of nothing,
When thought's in short supply,

A poet is the truest friend,
Gives their heart,
Asks nothing in return,
Shares the things that make you laugh,
Shares the things that burn.

A poet is a traveller,
Sets a course,
Takes you to a distant place,
They only need a pen, some time,
A page, and all its space.

The Mermaid's Purse

I spied a mermaid's purse,
As I walked across the beach one day,
Nestled in a rock pool,
Beneath a sky of marble grey,
And there beside the empty sands,
And the sleepless ocean's restless din,
Carefully, I looked inside,
To see what wonders lay within.

A song to lift a sailor's soul,
Coloured like a rainbow,
Sunlight breaking through the clouds,
Eagle-winged and soaring high,
Star-tinged glow and millpond moon,
To light a dark and dreary sky.

A kiss to win a reckless heart,
Gentle as a baby's sigh,
Blossom scent from cherry trees,
As fragrant as the noble rose,
Lingering like morning dew,
To take away the weight of woes.

A chance to change a troubled course,
Crystal glow and diamond clear,
Glinting gold within the stream,
Footsteps out the lion's den,
As precious as a dragon's hoard,
To help the hopeless start again.

A thought to ease a weary mind,
Warm like late autumnal fires,
Refreshing like a summer breeze,
Vibrant like the winter frost,
Springtime soft like daffodils,
To give new strength to all that's lost.

I spied a mermaid's purse,
As I walked across the beach one day,
Nestled in a rock pool,
Beneath a sky of marble grey.

The Pea

"Mother, mother, what's for tea?"
"A pea, my son, a garden pea."
"Just one pea, a single pea?
But that is not enough for me!"

"One pea, my son, is wholesome food,
But as you've been so very rude,
I'll now give you just half a pea,
And that is all you'll get for tea!"

"Half a pea? Just half a pea?
Surely, Mother, you can see,
That half a pea, just half a pea,
Is nowhere near enough for me!"

"Half a pea is full of life,
But as you've moaned and caused me strife,
You'll only have a single quarter –
Full of goodness, full of water!"

"A quarter, Mother, is much worse.
Can we take this in reverse?
I'm sorry for my attitude,
I'm sorry that I was so rude …

I’m sorry for my dreadful greed,
A single pea will suit indeed.”
“I’m sorry son, I’m sorry too,
Have more than one, in fact, have two!”
“Thank you, Mom, you’re very kind.”
“It’s quite okay, I do not mind!”

My Hope

Breezy sunny days,
Woodland haze,
Seaside fresh,
Bright blue sky,
Fluffy clouds
And that's my hope for summer.

Daffodils and tulips,
Candyfloss blossom,
Bluebell glades
Morning's light,
Life reborn
And that's my hope for spring.

Horse chestnut trees with conkers aplenty
Leaves of gold and russet,
Jack-a-lantern windowpanes,
Bonfire smoke,
Harvest and hay bales,
And that's my hope for autumn.

Snowy lanes and candlelight,
Fires crackle,
Stockings wait,
A peaceful sigh,
Goodwill abounds,
And that's my hope for winter.

A questioning mind,
Calm patience,
Imagination's rainbow,
A kind word,
An explorer's heart,
And that's my hope for me.

Fair winds,
Set course,
Gentle seas,
Sturdy sails,
Solid craft,
And that's my hope for you.

Smiling faces,
Helping hands,
Happy routines,
Unexplored paths,
Tackled problems,
And that's my hope for life.

Summer through the Seasons

Dragonfly and damselfly,
Painted Lady butterfly,
Watch them gently flutter by,
Upon a summer day.

Twirling leaves come falling down,
Coat the pavements of the town,
Fire glow and russet gown,
When summer goes away.

Frozen streams by water mills,
Snowy lanes and morning chills,
Icy frost on windowsills,
With summer nowhere near.

Lambs a-bleating, meadows green,
Daffodils can now be seen,
Branches pink with blossomed sheen,
And summer almost here.

Enter the Circus

"Come enter the circus!" the ringmaster cries,
With his waxy moustache and his black dapper hat,
And excitement that glows in his eyes.

"Listen one, listen all, hear the calliope call!

Come watch the gymnasts tumble,
Come watch the trampoline,
Where acrobats jump higher,
Than a person's ever been.

See aerial contortionists,
Who launch from each trapeze,
The circus is the only place,
You see sights such as these.

Roll up! Roll up! And see the stilts,
Where men walk ten feet high,
Then twenty feet and thirty feet,
They almost reach the sky!

Then up above and higher still,
The tightrope stretches out,
Come see the 'Walk of Wonder'
Come see the 'Walk of Doubt!'

Join in the buffoonery,
Wipe away your frowns,
With juggling tomfoolery,
And laugh-inducing clowns.

Come see the Human Cannonball
With not one trace of fear,
Will he be a cloud of dust?
Will he disappear?

The man who swallows silver swords –
That have the sharpest blade,
Watch in utter disbelief,
This shocking escapade!

The strongman who lifts anvils,
The girl who breathes out flame,
The Knife Thrower, who blindfolded,
Excels with every aim.

Come behold the conjurer,
His subtle art that teases,
The marvel of his magic craft,
An act that always pleases.

See the Lion Tamer's nerve,
She'll enter in the cage,
Then pacify the 'King of Beasts'
And soothe his snarling rage!

Yes, come and see the circus,
Come and see the show,
Step into the Big Top,
You will not want to go!

Come enter the circus!" the ringmaster cries,
With his waxy moustache and his black dapper hat,
And excitement that glows in his eyes.

Shh! Don’t Wake the Baby!

Shh! Don’t wake the baby,
She is snoring fast asleep,
Shh! Don’t wake the baby,
Do not make a peep!

Along comes the elephant:

“I won’t wake the baby,
I’ll be quiet like a mouse,
I’ll knot my trunk and watch my feet,
Whilst moving in the house.”

Along comes the snake:

“I won’t wake the baby,
I’ll be quiet like a mouse,
Just watch thissss; I’ll hold my hissss,
Whilsssst moving in the house.”

Along comes the kangaroo:

“I won’t wake the baby,
I’ll be quiet like a mouse,
I’ll put a stop to every hop,
Whilst moving in the house.”

Along comes the cat:

“I won’t wake the baby,
I’ll be quiet like a mouse,
Just for her, I’ll pause my purr,
Whilst moving in the house.”

Along comes the mouse:

“I won’t wake the baby,
I really promise that,
I won’t wake the baby...
ARGH – JEEPERS! THERE’S A CAT!

Cat, cat, cat, cat, CAT!!!!
I’M DONE FOR!” cried the mouse,
And he clattered every object,
As he ran throughout the house.

Shh! Don’t wake the baby!
But baby woke – too bad –
“Waaaahhh!” the baby screamed,
The baby sounded sad.

Mouse, you woke the baby!
You should have taken care,
Mouse you woke the baby,
And that simply wasn't fair.

We'll have to have new rules now,
When moving through the house,
Be as quiet as an elephant,
A kangaroo,
A snake,
A cat,
But don't be like a mouse!

Nasheroo the Crocodile

Have you heard of a sneaky crocodile -
The one called Nasheroo?
He sleeps with one eye open,
And he waits for me and you.
He wallows in a bath of mud,
And sunbathes in the heat –
But the time that he likes best of all,
Is when it's time to eat.

He's partial to some monkey tail,
Zebra, hare, gazelle,
He'll nibble on some wildebeest,
He chews giraffe as well.
Hyenas never laugh at him,
For their legs just turn to jelly,
They know that if they come to close,
They'll end up in his belly.

The brave lion may rule the kingdom,
Yet this isn't really true.
For King Leo shakes with fear,
When he thinks of Nasheroo.
He's the champion of cunning,
The master of deceit.
His favoured snacks are human beings,
Now there's a special treat.

His teeth are sharp as razor blades,
His claws contain such force.
He gobbles up his helpless prey,
And never shows remorse.
He'll chew your legs, your feet and knees,
And disregard your moans.
He'll munch and crunch your fingertips,
Whilst spitting out your bones.

So, when you near the water's edge,
Beware of where you tread.
He looks as though he's dreaming,
But remember what I've said.
You may never quite be watching him –
But he's always watching you.
The crocodile that no one likes –
The nasty Nasheroo.

Apples and Pears

Apples and pears, I saw on the stairs,
A harvest mouse singing of glory,
Peaches and plums, he played on the drums,
And hummed such a wonderful story,
Lemons and limes, he chimed out in rhymes,
He seemed to have marvellous speaking,
Damsons and dates, he called to the saints,
But much of it sounded like squeaking.

Noah

Forty days and forty nights,
And all it's done is rain!
I'm getting slightly wet my Lord,
Might I just complain?
No Lord? Well, that's fine with me,
I'll gladly steer this ark,
Through the ocean sea tsunamis,
Though the sky is very dark!

Gosh this ship is smelly now,
With sweat and foul manure!
I'm feeling slightly sick my Lord,
Are you really sure?
Yes my Lord? Well, that's okay,
I guess the scent is fine,
With the skunks and all the stink bugs,
And the pair of sloppy swine!

I'm feeling very tired now,
A panda's in my bed,
Will you conjure me a hammock Lord,
To rest my weary head?
No Lord? That's no problem,
I can sleep upon the floor,
I'm sure the many splinters,
Will not bother me at all!

Is there far to go now Lord?
I feel an awful chill,
I've congestion on my chest my Lord,
Is this your righteous will?
Yes my Lord? Affirmative?
Well, that's just plain swell,
Don't worry Lord, I'll carry on,
But man, I feel unwell!

Did we have to bring the porcupines?
They make me feel so glum!
I think I have two dozen spikes,
Lodged within my bum!
Yes my Lord? Very well,
That's just sweet and dandy,
But I wish I'd brought some tweezers Lord -
Right now they would be handy!

I hope you're warm up there Lord,
For it's not so hot down here!
You are Lord? Well, that's perfect,
It makes me want to cheer,
I'm very, very pleased for you,
So snug there up above,
But Lord, please get a move on now,
And quickly send that dove!

The Sandpit

When I was at the seaside,
On every holiday,
I had a very special spot,
Where I would sit and play.

That spot was called the sandpit,
And when I was so tiny,
With a spade and bucket by my side,
It's there where you would find me.

Beneath the shade of leafy trees,
The coastal breeze would blow,
On lazy summer afternoons,
It was the place to go.

For you could build a fortress,
Its turrets rising high,
And shells would glisten on its walls,
Underneath a joyful sky.

And in this new built kingdom,
Of lofty castles in the sand,
A moat would trickle form the sea,
To guard the realm and all the land.

And the people, made from pebbles,
Would be transformed from lumps of stone,
To soldiers, rulers, sailors,
With lives to live and hopes to own.

For two weeks, every August,
They'd find new breath again.
In the dominion of that sandpit,
Of golden shells and pebble men.

And still that sandpit stands today,
Though smaller than it seemed,
Where imagination had its lease,
And tranquil dreams were dreamed.

And though I am a giant now,
For that's the way of time,
Someday, my spirit will return,
To the province that was mine.

Queen Sapphire

Queen Sapphire (psychopath)
Chopped off heads, it made her laugh,
To see them roll upon the floor,
Was not enough, she wanted more,
And though it was an extra hassle,
She put up spikes outside her castle,
And had the heads (which looked dismayed),
Stuck on the spikes and then displayed,
And thus it was, it could be seen,
Queen Sapphire was quite mean.

She'd chop off heads of folk unknown,
She clapped when axes chopped through bone,
"Oh joy!" she cried, "It is so good,
To see the gore and all the blood,
Heads are ace, they look so nice,
Starring at me on their spikes."
But soon it was, she felt bereft,
She'd killed her subjects, few were left,
Apart from those Sapphire knew,
Her family, friends and teachers too!

Queen Sapphire shed a tear,
"I think," she said, with deepest fear,
"I need more heads so badly so,
I'll have to kill the folk I know.
'Teacher, teacher!' Queeny cried,
"Your time has come to die outside!"
"You what?" the kindly teacher said,
"You mean to say you want my head?
I taught you stuff, I educated!"
"ENOUGH!" Sapphire screamed frustrated,
"Choppy chop it's time to die,
Farewell my dearest teacher, bye!"

The teacher gave a nervous cough,
And soon his head went whizzing off,
Sapphire called, "I need another,
Head to chop, how 'bout it Mother?
Father too, and then my sisters,
Who both annoy me like sore blisters,
Choppy chop, it's very quick,
A minor cut, the slightest nick,
Before you even close your eyes,
Your heads will fly throughout the skies,
And then they will be made perfection,
Stuck on spikes in my collection."

One chop, two chops, three chops, four,
Sapphire's family were no more.
"Friends!" she called, "Oh friendsypoos,
I need your help; I have some news!

It's time to die! How great is that?
The axe must fall and go 'kersplat',
Upon your heads, upon your lives,
I do not use old swords or knives!"
"Please spare us!" all her friends made pleas,
They begged for mercy on their knees,
But choppy chop, they soon were gone,
And left remaining was just one.

Queen Sapphire all alone,
Sat upon her royal throne,
"All are gone," Sapphire wept,
"No heads to lose, there's no one left,
No heads to chop for me no more,
No heads a-rolling on the floor,
No choppy chop, oh why, oh why?
There's no one left to kill or die,
No choppy chop, it makes me mad,
I'm so upset and very sad."

And so, Sapphire went insane,
No choppy chop alarmed her brain,
No heads to cut and now I think,
She chops up carrots in her sink,
"Haha!" she laughs with crazy stare,
"I'll kill all carrots everywhere!"
So poor carrots be alarmed,
That bonkers queen will see you harmed,
She's potty and she cannot stop,
So, stay away or choppy chop!

The Moon in the Water

A little boy saw the moon within the millpond,
And thinking it imprisoned, he reached in
with his fishing net and tried to get it out,
But as he touched the water, it seemingly
broke into a thousand icy fragments,
And he ran home in tears believing
he had destroyed its silver essence.

He cried himself to sleep that night with
ocean salt tears and a guilt as heavy as lead,
For he pictured the world without the
beautiful maiden in her pearl-embroidered gown,
Who each night in the darkness, gave the dreamers hope
and the poets a ribbon of thoughtful verse,
Whilst wrapping all sweethearts in the
gentle embrace of her platinum arms.

It was the barking of the midnight fox
that stirred him from his pillow,
Hopelessly, he walked to his window to see its tail of
flame disappear into the shadows of the inky gloom,
And there, he noticed a faint trickle of a
nickel river beneath the resting daffodils,
He looked up,
And like the greatest gift of magic, the ghostly orb hung in the sky,
Watching all the world once more with its soft and glinting eye.

Ragamuffin

Ragamuffin, Ragamuffin,
Heart of straw and head of stuffin',
Does he know much? Next to nuffin',
Scarecrow, scarecrow, Ragamuffin.

Ragamuffin, Ragamuffin,
The red-tinged sky above is blushin',
The crows are squarkin' and a gushin',
Soldier-like stands Ragamuffin.

Ragamuffin, Ragamuffin,
Eyes are open, not a shuttin',
Crows are comin', stop 'em rushin',
Keep yer guard up, Ragamuffin!

Ragamuffin, Ragamuffin,
Losin' barley would be crushin',
We like the fields hushed and hushin',
Scarecrow, scarecrow, Ragamuffin.

The Chimney Sweep's World

Up amongst the chimney tops,
From rooftops, I gaze down,
And see the setting sun light up,
A sleepy London Town.

Crimson, pink and yellow,
Is the wash across the smoky sky,
Inky clouds like silhouettes,
Drifting like a peaceful sigh.

And in the far-off distance,
From the dome of great St Paul's,
The chiming bells sing out 'Sleep well',
With happy, tranquil calls.

And the final sunbeams glisten,
Like treasure through the darkened spires,
Whilst the gas lamps from the lanes below,
Glow like burning autumn fires.

And though my face is sooty,
And my clothes are worn and old,
Up here, amongst the angels,
My pleasure gleams like gold.

This is where my heart belongs:
Where pigeons roost and sleep,
You'll see my shadow dancing,
In the kingdom of the sweep.

Heidi

Heidi's always hiding,
Among the plants and trees,
Bemused by pretty butterflies,
Bewitched by bumble bees.
Her green eyes gaze from shadows,
They sparkle from the shade,
Two gemstones in the darkness,
Two spheres of shining jade.
Heidi's always hiding,
But not far does she roam,
For the garden is her sanctuary,
The flowers are her home.

The Garden Gnome

It's dusk now and the day is done,
The faded sun a dot of red,
The garden gnome now blinks his eyes,
And rather stiff, he turns his head.
He smokes upon his wooden pipe,
And glances t'ward the silent pond,
Where bathes the primrose fairy queen,
A sprite of whom he's very fond.
And though he never speaks to her,
He marvels at her silken wings,
And dreams of walking hand in hand,
Through leafy glades or mountain springs.

But he knows that this is not his fate,
For the job of any gnome,
Is to stay upon the garden lawn,
And guard the humble home,
Where he drinks the dew from autumn webs,
And sips the nectar of the rose,
Is thankful for the robin's song,
And loves the mud between his toes,
But, be sure, you'll never see him,
No glimpse or single peep,
For this man of stone, he only moves,
When we are fast asleep.

Conkers

In the quiet of the churchyards,
When autumn wears its russet gown,
Amid the fallen, scarlet leaves,
There's treasure shining smooth and brown!

At three o'clock, the school bell chimes,
And eager children swarm like bees,
For conkers call like nectar,
From the dappled light of ancient trees.

Such busy hands, as deft as thieves,
And faster than the steaming train,
Pockets filled and off they go,
To homes a-waiting down the lane.

Some to jars of vinegar,
Some to varnish from the sheds,
Some to bake inside old stoves,
But all to dance on shoelace threads.

And by the lichen gravestones,
Once happy raiders leave the scene,
A calmness in the evening haze,
And sleeping souls are left serene.

The Bat who was Scared of the Sky

Deep in the dark,
Of a big, old cave,
Lived a small, wee bat,
Who was not that brave.
He hung from the roof,
And he screwed up his eyes,
And he flat out refused,
To fly in the skies.

"It's awfully scary,"
He said to the bear,
"It's safer in here,
Than it would be out there,
For sometimes it rains,
And sometimes it hails!
And sometimes it blows
The most vicious of gales!"

"So true," said the bear,
"But it isn't all bad,
It's dreary in here,
And will make you feel sad,
The air is alive,
And there's much to be done,
Spread your wings little bat,
And go have some fun!"

"It's dreadfully creepy,"
The bat soon replied,
"For sometimes it snows,
When you venture outside,
And then there's the thunder,
And flashes of light,
It's perfect in here,
Where I snuggle up tight!"

"I see," said the bear,
"But what of the moon,
And the owls in the tree,
Who are singing their tune?
They belong to the night,
And bat, so do you,
Get out there and see,
It's the right thing to do!"

"But it's woefully eerie,"
The bat answered back,
"I'm fine where I am,
In the gloom and the black,
I'm best to avoid,
All the fog and the frost,
For out in the mist,
I am bound to get lost!"

"Indeed," said the bear,
(His voice very loud)
"But I'm having a date,
And three is a crowd,

So it's time you get out now,
It is best for your health,
If you don't move a muscle,
I'll eat you myself!"

"It's terribly strange,"
Said the bat in a flash,
"But I've had second thoughts,
Away I must dash!
Leaving appeals!
In fact, I can't wait!
I hope it goes well –
Good luck with the date!"

So off he then flew,
And what a surprise!
He beheld so much beauty,
In his two little eyes,
The splendour of stars,
As he rode on the breeze,
And the silvery light,
On the sparkling seas.

Oh what a joy,
Through the ribbons of cloud,
"This is amazing!"
He cried out aloud!
"Not a raindrop in sight,
Indeed, it's all fine!
I'm the king of the sky,
And the world is all mine!"

As for the bear,
(Who had told a small lie)
"I did not have a date,"
He said with a sigh,
"But I wanted some sleep,
I'm in need of my rest,
And the little bat snores,
And it's sort of a pest!

Bow now I have space!
There is no need to groan!
I can stretch out in comfort,
Now I am alone!
It's peaceful and tranquil,
It really is swell!
Goodnight!"
He then yawned,
And he slept rather well!

Minty

I had a sheep called Minty,
He was my final hope,
Porky, Beefy – both had gone,
Minty helped me cope.
I used to stroke his silky fleece,
He used to lick my hand,
He used to, 'till he disappeared,
I just don't understand.

"Tell me why they hate me Dad –
Do I stink of poo?
I want to hear an oink or bleat,
I want to hear a moo.
Do I look alarming Dad?
Is something out of place?
I thought that I was normal, Dad,
Why did they leave this place?"

"Minty wanted better things,
He disliked country air,
Perhaps he went to London Town,
I know it seems unfair.
But trust me son, it's not your fault,
Now go and get a bowl –
Your frail nerves need nourishment –
I've made a casserole."

Again, Dad reassured me,
For now, things seemed okay –
"How did you make this casserole?"
No answer – "Dad, I say –
How did you make this casserole?"
Said Dad, "With lots of stuff,
But to be honest, I don't like it son,
I think I've had enough.

This meal has given me jaw ache son,
The stew is full of gristle,
In short, it's not enjoyable,
Like eating Scottish thistle!"
"Don't worry Dad, for now instead,
We'll speak and chat and talk,
Why did Minty take a hike?
Why did Minty walk?"

"Perhaps he's gone to fly a plane,
Perhaps he's got a job –
In truth, I never liked him son –
I thought he was a slob.
He isn't worth the upset son,
Your friendship was a duff,
Minty was too bitter son,
Minty was too tough.

Minty was a bad sheep,
But those memories… we'll savour,
I know that his departure son,
Has left a nasty flavour,
Your tears will make me weep as well,
Don't cry, you'll fill a moat,
And besides, I have already got,
A lump stuck in my throat!"

For You

For you, I'd climb every step of Jacob's ladder,
I'd confront the lions in their den,
I'd build the ark amid the drought,
I'd do them all, and all again.

I'd find the beauty in the beast,
I'd spin all straw to strands of gold,
I'd cross the bridge and face the troll,
I'd write the stories left untold.

I'd count up to infinity,
I'd solve a crime without a clue,
Upon the shore, I'd stop the tide,
I'd do them all, and all, for you.

Oodles of Noodles

Eat oodles of noodles,
They're awfully nice,
Better than pasta,
Or parsnips with rice,
Better than strudels,
And slices of citrus,
More soothing than honey,
Or fresh eucalyptus,
Feed them to poodles,
Or have them yourself,
Good for the soul,
And good for your health,
Play on your plate,
Arrange them in doodles,
You'll never go wrong,
With oodles of noodles,
No never go wrong,
With oodles of noodles,
No never go wrong,
With oodles of noodles.
Oodles of noodles,
Oodles of noodles,
No never go wrong,
With oodles of noodles.

I’m a Skunk and I Stink

I’m a skunk,
And I stink,
And I hate it,
I’m a skunk,
And I stink,
And it’s sad,
I’m a skunk and I stink,
I think there’s a link,
I’m a skunk and I stink,
And it’s bad!

I’m a skunk,
And I smell,
Pretty awful,
I’m a skunk,
And I smell,
Like a loo,
I’m a skunk and I smell,
And it’s not very swell,
I’m a skunk and I smell,
Like poo.

I'm a skunk
And I pong,
And I'm sorry,
I'm a skunk,
And I pong,
I regret,
I'm a skunk and I pong,
I realise it's wrong,
I'm a skunk and I pong,
And I sweat!

I'm a skunk,
And I whiff,
Mega badly,
I'm a skunk,
And I whiff,
It's a shock!
I'm a skunk and I whiff,
It's not just a myth,
I'm a skunk and I whiff,
Like a sock.

I'm a skunk,
And I reek,
It's a problem!
I'm a skunk,
And I reek,
Oh gosh!
I'm a skunk and I reek,
And trust me, it's bleak,
I'm a skunk and I reek,
So I'll wash!

The Dance of the Wind

"Hop, skip, jump," said Wind,
To the leaves upon the ground,
And he swirled them in an autumn dance,
Around, around, around.

How eagerly those leaves did fly,
Their crimsons caught the light of day,
Toward the sun, up in the sky,
Away, away, away.

Upon the gust a-bustling,
Yellow dresses, evening haze,
The orange sunset rustling,
Ablaze, ablaze, ablaze.

"Swoop, fall, glide," said Wind,
And he thought to leave them then,
So, they spiralled down to kiss the earth,
Again, again, again.

And there they rested dizzily,
Their pulses racing from their flight,
Their hearts and minds and senses,
Alight, alight, alight.

But the Wind, he did not linger,
To distant shores, he quickly flew,
And he called behind across the sea,
"Adieu, adieu, adieu."

When

When the road you walk is fruitless,
And your rainbow fades away,
When your window opens up,
To reveal a sky of grey,
And on looking out, it stays the same,
Each day, a dismal day,

When the words you speak are smothered,
And the birds all take to flight,
When the flowers in your garden,
Are stole away each night,
And the glowing warmth of autumn,
Pales to winter's white,

When the faith you feel is shattered,
And your visions turn to stone,
When your kingdom starts to crumble,
And you're left without a throne,
When you're holding on to nothing,
As it's all you have to own,

When the love you share is broken,
And your soul begins to crack,
When the only way is forward,
But you're set on turning back,
And your heart's a lonely hunter -
A wolf without a pack,

When the dreams you dream are dashed,
And truth bites sharp like fire,
When the path you're on is tangled,
With weeds of thorn and briar,
And you need to cross the precipice,
But cannot walk the wire,

Then take your spade, dig deeper,
Take your time, think more,
Take the hands of those you trust,
Holder tighter than before,
Do not hide yourself away,
Take down every wall,

Leave yourself more open,
Never close your door,
You may have lost some battles,
But you will not lose the war,
You'll always find a lighthouse,
Awaiting on some shore,

So, gather up your courage,
Hear the lion roar,
Haven't got yourself a map?
Nowhere to explore?
Then be your own cartographer,
Take your pen ...
and draw.

Rest and be Thankful

Rest and be thankful,
For rain and for sun,
For wheat and for barley,
And the day that is done,
For the bleating of sheep,
And the lowing of cows,
For the shovel and scythe,
And the horse leading ploughs.

Rest and be thankful,
For sleep you have won,
For the strength in your bones,
And the day just begun,
For the store in the pantry,
For the milk in the churn,
For the seeds in the soil,
And the seasons that turn.

Rest and be thankful,
For acres of land,
For the air to be breathed,
Now the day is at hand,
For the flowers in the meadow,
For the hives and their yield,
And for the harvest that is waiting,
In the orchards and the field.

Church Mouse

I dance in the light of the stained-glass windows,
The sun illuminating the cold stone floor in rainbows,
And I feel the brightness of a springtime dawn in the scatterings of yellow,
And the sensation of the meadow grass in lovely rays of green,
In blue, I think of running streams and the rivers of my distant youth,
Whilst lingering in poppy shade amid the glow of red.

I am old now and must seek the warmth I find indoors,
In amongst the wooden pews, I take my daily bread,
I find wonder in the emptiness and company in sleeping souls,
There is peace within the stillness,
And tranquillity surrounds the tombs,
A sacredness descends as I watch the calm on faces,
Whilst I live amongst the dead.

Sometimes, on a Sunday, the wooden doors will open wide,
It is no intrusion really for I listen to the words,
I do not understand them, but they have the sound of beauty,
Like the birdsong at the break of day,
Or the wind which rustles through the idle reeds on riverbanks,
Or the babble of the youthful brook,
So long before it meets the sea.

Soon most people fade away and I spy a single man,
His hair is white and skin ripples in gentle folds across his brow,
He almost smiles sadly in his collar of moonlight white,
I venture near, though he does not see,
I do not fear as I sense no harm,
I contemplate with him,
Though he does not know.

The Spider and the Glider

A spider brought a glider for a flight above the town,
"Don't do it!" said his mother, "It's a
Long,
Long,
Long,
Way down.
You are VERY, VERY small, the sky is very high,
Spiders are supposed to crawl; they're not supposed to fly!"

But spider didn't listen; and he swooped from off a ledge,
And below him were the flowers and the grasses and the hedge.
"I'm flying!" sang the spider, "I'm flying, look at me!"
And as he went along his way, he met a bumble bee.

"Greetings!" said the bumble bee, "Beeeeeeeeee careful, beeeeeeeeee alert,
Beeeeeeeeee mindful of how far you go, or else you could get hurt.
You are VERY, VERY small, the sky is very high,
Spiders are supposed to crawl; they're not supposed to fly!"

But spider didn't listen; he carried on instead,
Below him were the garden and the patio and shed.
"I'm flying!" sang the spider, "How brilliant is that?"
And as he went along his way, he met a horseshoe bat.

“Greetings!” said the horseshoe bat, “I think that you should stop,
The wind is getting stronger and you wouldn’t want to drop,
You are VERY, VERY small, the sky is very high,
Spiders are supposed to crawl; they’re not supposed to fly!”

But spider didn’t listen; he glided with such glee,
And below were the meadow and the woodland and the sea.
“I’m soaring!” sang the spider, “Just watch me as I go!”
And as he went along his way, he met a hooded crow.

“Greetings!” said the hooded crow, “Caaaawww crikey, you’re at risk!
The clouds are getting greyer and the gusts are getting brisk,
You are VERY, VERY small, the sky is very high,
Spiders are supposed to crawl; they’re not supposed to fly!”

But spider didn’t listen, for he’d left behind his fear,
And below him were the lighthouse and the beaches and the pier,
“So thrilling!” sang the spider, “It’s the best time I have had!”
But a thunderstorm soon blocked his way, and thunderstorms are bad.

“Greetings!” said the thunderstorm, amid the squally scene,
“You shouldn’t be up here, how stupid you have been,
You are VERY, VERY small, the sky is very high,
Spiders are supposed to crawl; they’re not supposed to fly!”

The lightening flashed, the thunder roared, the gales grew and grew,
The spider gave a cry for help, his glider split in two,
And,
Down,
Down,
Down,

The spider fell,
From out the blackened skies,
"Soon I will be SQUISHED and SQUASHED!" he said and shut his eyes.

Down,
Down,
Down,
The spider fell,
As fast, as fast could go,
But what was this? The bumble bee, the horseshoe bat and crow!
They sped toward the falling dot; each grasped a tiny hand,
And soon they had delivered him, in safety, back to land.

"Thank you!" said the spider and he praised their splendid wings,
"You fly quite exquisitely; you're meant to do such things!
But I am VERY, VERY small, the sky is very high,
From now, I'll stick to spinning webs,
AND
PROMISE
Not to fly!"

Jack Frost

I am the artist who paints the world white,
I am the thief stealing warmth from the night,
I am the conjurer, bringing delight,
When the glow of the autumn is lost.

I am the prince with the icicle crown,
I am the poet of crystal renown,
I am the phantom who sneaks through the town,
And the people, they call me Jack Frost.

Elves Cannot Have Presents

"Elves cannot have presents,"
That's what her mother said,
As little baby Clementine,
Was tucked inside her bed,
"You must never give an elf a gift,
For they can only give,
By law they're bound not to receive,
As long as they shall live!"
Little baby Clementine,
Had eyes which opened wide,
As her mother's tale continued,
And the snow fell thick outside.

"No, elves cannot have presents,
And those who break the rule,
Are thrown within a dungeon,
With a chamber Arctic cool,
In the middle of The Great Unknown,
They pass away their time,
Reflecting on their errors,
And repenting of their crime:
By day, they're put to work,
Mining frost flakes out of stone,
In the Mountains of Forgetfulness,
Abandoned and alone.

There's worse to come, my darling girl,
For if a flake is chipped,
In a moment of complacency,
When a careless hand has slipped,
You are made to eat a lump of coal,
And sip from frozen streams,
There's no release by light of day,
And no escape in dreams,
You wear a single pebble,
Which forms a chilling threat,
You will remember always.
You simply can't forget.

And when your days are over,
And you cry your final groans,
The bear of the Forsaken Cave,
Will carry off your bones,
And the pebble from around your neck,
Will crumble in the breeze,
Do not give elves a present,
To avoid fates such as these!
And now my darling Clementine,
I bid to you, goodnight,
Sleep well my precious, precious girl,
Don't let the ice bear bite!"

The Stories We Tell

I am the glass slipper,
Left on the staircase,
By the girl who dared to dream.
The story I tell is of hatred that hinders,
Magic from ashes,
And sparkle from cinders.

I am the mirror cracked,
Broken by the hand of a vengeful queen,
Who came undone.
The story I tell is of vanity's fall,
To the purest of hearts and the fairest of all.

I am the needle on the spinning wheel,
Pricked by the finger of the princess,
Bound by fate.
The story I tell is of cold-hearted schemes,
The kiss of true love and a rescue from dreams.

I am the shard of frost,
Embedded in the warmest heart,
Unleashed by the soul,
Who could not contain her fury.
The story I tell is of a hand in a glove,
And the coldest of ice,
That was melted by love.

I am the tangled lock of hair,
The sunlight that I once contained,
Lost as the scissors cut away my length.
The story I tell is of a witch and her power,
A damsel, a prince and the height of a tower.

I am the smuggled diamond,
Robbed by the forty bandits,
Gleaming in the darkness,
Of a dank and dreary cave.
The story I tell (for he who believes)
Is of greed and good fortune,
Twixt chancers and thieves.

We are the objects,
Conjured in the minds,
On imagination's journey by the ones who hold a pen.
The stories we tell,
No scales can measure,
We endure beyond eternity,
And exceed the price of treasure.

Let's Go Hunt for Moondrops

Let's go hunt for moondrops,
In the silver syrup of the night,
Me and you: hand in hand,
Between the trees and weaves of light.

Let us take the winter path,
Where breaths forms crystals in the air,
And snowflakes paint the shadowlands,
And softly kiss the branches bare.

To a place around a corner lost,
Where the frost has claimed the sleeping stream,
And wrapped it in a shawl of ice,
To soothe it in its tranquil dream.

Together we will venture,
Through the shimmers of the broken dark,
Among the ribbons of the stars,
That glow upon the ancient bark.

Yes, let's go hunt for moondrops,
Far below the twinkle skies,
In a secret woodland hollow,
Where I'll find them dancing in your eyes.

Cloud Gazing

Lying back on meadow grass,
An absent-minded stare,
We watch the cotton clouds drift past,
Each dancing in the air.

They paint a thousand pictures,
Of beasts and ancient wonders,
Of angels, swans and fairy wings,
Of pirate ships and plunders.

Their colours show so many moods,
With yellow pinks of morning,
Cotton white on seas of blue,
Or heavy grey when warning.

Some look as light as whipped-up cream,
Soft feathers floating high,
Whilst others hang with droopy heads,
Too heavy for the sky.

Lying back on meadow grass,
But what can we expect?
A story for a moment,
But the page is turned the next.

The Glass Heart

The mist rolled in upon the moor,
And masked the heather's work of art,
Thick and dank, obscuring all,
You could not see where footpaths led,
Where sky would end or sea would start,
And hid within this ghostly veil,
And glad of its concealment,
A young man stood a-weeping,
Lost in his abandonment,
He clenched his broken heart.

He nursed those shattered pieces,
They cut his hands like jagged glass,
He wished to let them fall away,
Yet what is life without a heart?
He needed them, he had to heal,
The slightest chance this pain could pass,
Must drive him on,
For in his eyes there still shone hope,
A flicker of redemption,
That glowed like polished brass.

So maybe it was providence,
That in the early hours of night,
The woodland nymph Rhiannon,
With eyes as blue as damselfly,
Lips as red as raspberries,
And clad in seashell white,
Took pity on the stranger,
And sang to him in fairy tongue,
With melodies that soothed his pain,
And eased his troubled plight.

And so it was the faintest glow,
The shards of glass began to gleam,
When stirred from sleep,
The young man woke,
With abstract thoughts soon more distinct,
Like rivers from a stream,
Had he walked the hills the night before,
Or ventured there within his mind,
And in some distant dream?

He glanced upon the casket,
Where the debris of his heart was stored,
Perceiving now a second chance,
To mend the shattered treasure,
To forget the unrequited love,
That pierced him like a sword,
To think of fair Rhiannon,
Waiting on that lonely moor,
The healer of his sorrows,
And the keeper of his hoard.

For only sweet Rhiannon,
Had shown the skill to sooth despair:
He'd sought the help of others,
To fuse those damaged segments,
Enchantments of the sorcerer,
The surgeon's craft and care,
The blacksmith's skilled dexterity,
But none had been successful,
And now, against the fairy nymph,
Their work could not compare.

No spell can heal a broken heart,
Its essence is too pure,
Beyond the touch of magic,
Too complex for the surgeon's knife,
Resistant to the worker's art,
It cannot long endure –
Instead it must be cradled,
Bandaged by some wholesome faith,
That fortitude and fortune,
Will grant a subtle cure.

Thus to the windswept hilltops,
A fervent hunt along each vale,
He searched to find Rhiannon,
Yet despite his countless footsteps,
He never saw her presence,
And his quest was never finished,
But determined not to fail,
The years saw him continue,
Every morning filled with hope,
He'd find his Holy Grail.

He grew to love those well-walked paths,
And breathe the fragrant air,
And his heart got ever stronger,
For his burden was a happy one,
And something he could bear,
For in every seashell on the shore,
As damsels hovered by the brook,
In every growing raspberry,
He found Rhiannon there.

The Night Before Christmas when Rudolph had Fleas

"T'was the night before Christmas and all through the house,
Not a creature was stirring, not even a louse,
Well, that is all wrong and it's just a big lie,
Come Rudolph and listen – I'll let you know why!

See Rudolph, old mucker, old matey, old bean,
In the house things were stirring, those things were unseen,
I'll go a bit further and be more exact,
I shall tell you the truth and relate every fact.

For Rudolph, those things, which were stirring around,
Were not in the air, they were not on the ground,
They were not in the stockings, or stuffed up the flue,
No Rudolph, those things, were all stirring on you!

I'd got all the presents and I'd filled up my sack,
I'd gone for the harness to strap to your back,
But then what should fill the full gaze of my eyes?
But the worst of all horrors – an awful surprise!

I shrank back dumbfounded – I reached for a book,
I got out my spyglass and took a long look,
Then Rudolph, poor Rudolph I fell to my knees,
Good golly, good gracious, my Rudolph has fleas!

The presents were waiting; those sacks were filled high,
The sleigh was all polished and prepped up to fly,
Oh Rudolph, oh Rudolph, what have you been doing?
The night is upon us! Our time is ensuing!

If we stay in the grotto, just think of the mess,
The pain and the anguish, the hurt and distress –
It's nigh on disaster – I'm very afraid,
If we don't do our duties, I will not be paid!

Two million pounds I earn for this chore –
And now 'cause of you, I won't get any more,
Oh Rudolph, oh Rudolph, you shabby old thing,
I cannot go bankrupt; I must have my bling!

Dasher's gone lame, and Blitzen can't see,
Oh why do all bad things just happen to me?
Cupid is love struck and Comet's burned out,
Both Prancer and Vixen are riddled with gout.

Donner got poisoned by mouldy kebab,
Dancer's depressed and has gone to rehab!
We don't have an option – we'll have to get by,
Let's strap on your saddle and take to the sky!"

Narrator:

Thus Santa and Rudolph set unto their task,
The clouds hid the face of the moon like a mask,
The snowflakes fell softly and sank to the ground,
The earth was all silent and gave not a sound…

I remember it well as I lay in my bed,
A thud hit the roof and I propped up my head,
I rushed to the window and heard a hushed voice –
It spoke of regret and an absence of choice…

Santa:

"Oh Rudolph, oh Rudolph, I'm crawling with lice,
It's wretched, it's awful, it's not very nice,
And now 'cause of you and your bad infestation,
Fleas will take hold in the world's every nation!"

Narrator:

Then quick as a flash down the chimney he sprang,
He came to the bottom and crashed with a bang,
Soon out he emerged with bewildering pace,
And wiped off the soot from his guilt-ridden face.

His eyes, how they watered, the fleas were on him!
In an instant I knew that my chances were slim,
As the wee little blighters jumped off of his beard,
And leapt toward me in a way that I feared…

He dropped off the presents and turned on his heels,
And cried out, "I'm sorry for all your ordeals!"
Then as I stood scratching, as quick as a horse,
He leapt back on Rudolph and went to his course –

I hurried outdoors and shook my clenched fist,
I took up my rifle but sadly I missed,
And I heard him exclaim as he drove out of sight,
"Merry Christmas to all – hope the fleas do not bite!"

The Traveller's Carol

On this path we travel again,
On the road to Bethlehem,
Follow the star that hangs in the skies,
See the wonder held in our eyes,
Ho hey, on our way,
On our way to Bethlehem,
Ho hey, on our way,
A king is born today!

Lambs we bring to offer our love,
To praise the one who came from above,
Silken fleece as soft as the snows,
To cradle him wherever he goes,
Ho hey, on our way,
On our way to Bethlehem,
Ho hey, on our way,
A king is born today!

Incense, gold and fragrance of myrrh,
No threat to us will ever deter,
For on we go to offer our praise,
To He who rules the rest of our days,
Ho hey, on our way,
On our way to Bethlehem,
Ho hey, on our way,
A king is born today!

Out of heaven, down to the earth,
We sing a song to worship His birth,
Halos shine by moon in the night,
But only one can offer the light,
Ho hey, on our way,
On our way to Bethlehem,
Ho hey, on our way,
A king is born today!

Ho hey, on our way,
On our way to Bethlehem,
Ho hey, on our way,
A king is born today!

A Kiss in Haste

A princess and frog,
Romantically kissed,
Said the princess to frog,
"How could I resist?
But now I'm downhearted,
And in need of a rinse,
As you're still just a frog,
And I wanted a prince!"

A Farewell

The year has much to carry,
As it meets its final day,
It gathers up its knapsack,
Props it on its shoulder,
Takes a final glance,
And slowly moves away.

So many thoughts and memories,
Are bound in cotton sheets:
The triumphs and the hardships,
The laughter and the tears,
It bears them all the same,
As it walks the lamplit streets.

Then climbing up a distant hill,
Its time is coming soon,
It sits upon the summit,
Beneath the stars which twinkle,
And then slowly disappears,
Neath the shimmer of the moon.

The Ghost of Gressingham Hall

The ghost of a Georgian at Gressingham Hall,
Lurks within pictures and cracks in the wall.

The ghost of a Georgian at Gressingham Hall,
Lurks within pictures and cracks in the wall,
He wears a white wig that's incredibly tall!

The ghost of a Georgian at Gressingham Hall,
Lurks within pictures and cracks in the wall,
He wears a white wig that's incredibly tall!
And powders his face with a brush very small.

The ghost of a Georgian at Gressingham Hall,
Lurks within pictures and cracks in the wall,
He wears a white wig that's incredibly tall!
And powders his face with a brush very small,
Puts rouge on his lips that is meant to enthral!

The ghost of a Georgian at Gressingham Hall,
Lurks within pictures and cracks in the wall,
He wears a white wig that's incredibly tall!
And powders his face with a brush very small,
Puts rouge on his lips that is meant to enthral,
Then sings to his lady to dance at the ball.

The ghost of a Georgian at Gressingham Hall,
Lurks within pictures and cracks in the wall,
He wears a white wig that's incredibly tall!
And powders his face with a brush very small,
Puts rouge on his lips that is meant to enthral,
Then sings to his lady to dance at the ball,
But there comes no reply save the sound of the squall.

The ghost of a Georgian at Gressingham Hall,
Lurks within pictures and cracks in the wall,
He wears a white wig that's incredibly tall!
And powders his face with a brush very small,
Puts rouge on his lips that is meant to enthral,
Then sings to his lady to dance at the ball,
But there comes no reply save the sound of the squall,
Which is simply the wind saying nothing at all.

The ghost of a Georgian at Gressingham Hall,
Lurks within pictures and cracks in the wall,
He wears a white wig that's incredibly tall!
And powders his face with a brush very small,
Puts rouge on his lips that is meant to enthral,
Then sings to his lady to dance at the ball,
But there comes no reply save the sound of the squall,
Which is simply the wind saying nothing at all,
For there's no one around to answer the call.

The ghost of a Georgian at Gressingham Hall,
Lurks within pictures and cracks in the wall,
He wears a white wig that's incredibly tall!
And powders his face with a brush very small,
Puts rouge on his lips that is meant to enthral,
Then sings to his lady to dance at the ball,
But there comes no reply save the sound of the squall,
Which is simply the wind saying nothing at all,
For there's no one around to answer the call,
Of the ghost of the Georgian at Gressingham Hall.

Mount Pleasant

Stuart, Stevens, Webb and Brierley,
Were almost sure but not entirely,
Not entirely, you can see,
Is pretty close to certainty,
Pretty close is somewhere near,
A place that's far away from here,
Exactly where, I cannot tell,
It's not a region I know well!

Partridge, grouse, quail and pheasant,
On a journey to Mount Pleasant,
Roll a dice, odds and evens,
For Brierley, Stuart, Webb and Stevens,
Off they went down several tracks,
With knapsacks spread upon their backs.

With barley clenched within his mouth,
Stuart ran towards the south,
Met a Phoenix on the way,
Who didn't have a lot to say,
The ink is black, the page is white,
Through sunshine hot and moon-glow bright.

Thinking that the way was best,
Stevens walked towards the west,

Saw a sphinx and shouted “Hi!”
But never got a strong reply,
One more step through autumn days,
Through fog and mist and cloud and haze.

Deciding that she would step forth,
Brierley skipped towards the north,
Spied a mermaid in the sea,
Who did not wish for company,
An oiled lamp and kum ba yah,
Through thunder-rain, beneath a star.

Gulping down a sardine feast,
Webb then bounced towards the east,
Came across a unicorn,
Who tried to jab him with her horn,
A knight with spurs and morning breaks,
Through blizzard storms and snowy flakes.

Tides would flow and tides would ebb,
For Stevens, Brierley, Stuart, Webb
One with poppies, one with roses,
One with pretty primrose poses,
One held tulips in her hand,
Through ice and mud and bog and sand.

Moments passed since they departed,
Till they came to where they’d started,
Climbed the mountain, did not plummet,
All at once, they reached the summit!
Nestled close and all congruent,
Stevens, Brierley, Webb and Stuart.

In Bluebell Glades

In bluebell glades,
Within the wood,
All is calm,
And all is good,
And all at once,
My soul is free,
Upon my tide,
Beneath the tree.

In bluebell glades,
I sail away,
And lose myself,
Within the day,
And music from,
The tweeting birds,
Moves my heart,
To write these words.

Neptune – The Mystic

Hypnotic is my pendant,
As it drifts through waves of purple,
In the inky twilight velvet of an ocean still with grace,
A void of tranquil nothingness,
That seeps through tired, troubled minds,
A soothing, silky satin in the emptiness of space.

Let your thoughts run free like rain,
That trickle to an unknown realm,
Grow lighter as a wisp of air that wanders through the formless night,
Feel numbness take your weight away,
And lift your soul, now feather-like,
On uncertain notes of harmony towards a calm and tranquil light.

Hypnotic is my pendant,
As you leave behind your consciousness,
To a voyage of abstract wonder through forgotten fathomed skies,
And soundless is the trodden path,
As the echoes fade to stillness,
And the silence all around you is the land of lullabies.

Sing a Song of Riverbanks

Sing a song of riverbanks,
Swing for all you're worth,
Will you hit the water,
Or make it to the earth?
The rope is hanging from the tree,
Gather up your pride,
If you fall, you'll be soaked through,
So, reach the other side.

Sing a song of riverbanks,
Pooh Sticks in the stream,
The dappled sunlight through the trees,
Is like a summer dream.
Synchronise the dropping twigs,
Then just watch them go,
Racing onward to the sea,
Then where?
We do not know.

Sing a song of riverbanks,
Skimming stones for fun,
In the coolness of the evening,
When daytime's all but done.
Surface-skipping dynamos,
Miss them if you blink,
But close your eyes in awkwardness,
When they start to sink.

The Colours of Love

Love is red because it is like poppies – you wear it and will never forget,
Love is green because it is like the first buds of spring,
Love is yellow because it is like the warm glow of a buttercup,
Love is blue because it is like the swirling ocean torrent,
Love is white because it is like a blank page with unspoken words,
Love is black because it is like the deepest cavern waiting to be explored,
Love is orange because it is like the sunrise that brings hope of a new day,
Love is pink because it is like candyfloss waiting to be eaten,
Love is indigo because it is mysterious as the distant realms of an unknown world.

Lion, Scarecrow, Tin Man

Lion, scarecrow, tin man,
Courage, brains and heart,
If you could choose to have but one,
I wonder where you'd start.

For courage drives you onward,
To overcome a fear,
To speak up when the time is right,
To listen and to hear,
To take a calculated risk,
When winds of doubt do blow,
To test just what is possible,
And see how far you'll go.

Brains are glints of genius,
To learn from our mistakes,
To ride the train of wonderment,
And not apply the brakes,
To revel in the blazing light,
Of one creative spark,
To illuminate the minds of men,
And venture from the dark.

Hearts are understanding,
The keys to open doors,
To share a special moment,
And to say, “What’s mine is yours,”
They’re the bridge to feeling empathy,
The essence of the soul,
And though they can be broken,
They sparkle when they’re whole.

Lion, scarecrow, tin man,
Courage, brains and heart,
If you could choose to have but one,
I wonder where you’d start.

The Dragon's Lair

Tread you softly if you dare,
We walk within the dragon's lair,
Be thy brave and be thy bold,
Upon the hills of shining gold.
Scarcely breathing, on we creep,
Through the chasms of the deep,
With glowing walls of ruby red,
And emerald halls that lie ahead,
In opal dreams the lizard lies,
Soaring through his brimstone skies,
A lust that glows like amethyst,
Within his soul of topaz mist,
Stay away from everything,
The glowing chalice; shining ring,
The gleaming platter, sacred cup -
He'll wake with just the slightest touch,
So let us leave his amber path,
Or risk the flame of burning wrath.

Cardigan Square

I remember Cardigan Square,
The girl with the poppy sewn into her hair,
Sat on a bench in the summertime air,
As I was busy dreaming.

I pictured a church with a sweeping, long aisle,
The sun on her face and the warmth of her smile,
And lost in her eyes, I lingered a while,
Like diamonds, they were beaming.

But the touch of the breeze brought me back to myself,
Like a rogue in the darkness, it came with such stealth,
And with it, the loss of my fantasied wealth,
As it fell to reality's scheming.

The man with the glow of her love in his heart,
Her rising to greet him, like figures in art,
The blissful embrace which tore me apart,
As her ring in the sunlight was gleaming.

Yes, I remember Cardigan Square,
And the girl with the poppy sewn into her hair.

Precious Things

A boy named Jack took his sack,
To find precious gifts,
(Say one, say two, say three)
Over the hills and far away,
Where the opal moon shines bright like day,
To a land where the pixie fairies play,
On the shores of a sugar-pot sea.

"Tis a curious thing," spoke the Pixie King,
With a watchful eye,
(Say four, say five, say six)
"To stray so very far from home,
To take such footsteps as you roam,
To my palace, so fine, with its biscuit-tin dome,
And its wonders of magic-dust tricks."

"Now venture back, young master Jack,
Where your heart belongs."
(Say seven, say eight, say nine)
"A loving mommy's smiley glow,
A loving daddy's hug 'hello',
The words, 'We love you – hope you know!'
Are gifts more precious than mine."

A boy named Jack,
Took his sack,
(Count now one through ten)
Swift by the harbour and Cockle Shell Bay,
Where the daffodil sun shines bright on display,
And a smile, a hug and ‘I love you’ each day,
Are gifts given again and again.

QUANTOCK BELLE

Evening Run of the Quantock Belle

Standing on the distant hills,
Free and feeling fine,
Like the buzzards, we watched eagerly,
Our eyes transfixed upon the line,
We listened for the signal,
Our cameras aimed to take the shot,
Would it run on time this hour?
We held our nerve; we doubted not.

The sky, a watercolour blue,
That we should be so lucky!
The fields were washed with dappled light,
Each wispy cloud was cotton fluffy,
The shadows cast upon the field,
Longer with the evening haze,
And then the sound we'd waited for,
The whistle whined; we set our gaze.

Hear the rumble of the thunder,
Its wheels roll along the track,
Its inner fire burning,
Like a dragon scaled green and black,
Exhaling smoke in drifting coils,
That made their way up to the sky,
Marauding through the countryside,
The great steam train goes rushing by.

Fingers poised and there it is!
The engine fast approaches,
The funnel and the piston,
The passengers in coaches,
It passes in an instant,
And oh the awe and thrill!
It lasts beyond the moment,
When all is calm again and still.

The crickets start their chirping,
The birds begin to sing,
The breeze finds strength to blow again,
For it seemed that almost everything,
Paused in humble reverence,
Like the sunshine when the day is done,
As even nature holds its breath,
When the Quantock Belle goes on her run.

The Missing Thumb

There once was a cook
(I once read in a book)
Whilst cutting the carrots,
He misplaced the knife.
Now that was quite dumb,
For he sliced off his thumb,
And he felt rather thick,
So did not tell his wife.
But his wife was quite clever,
And she gasped, "Well I never –
What a rotten and bad thing to do!
You'd better think on,
Where your thumb might have gone –
Let's hope that it's not in the stew!"

Quickly the cook,
Took a jittery look,
In the carrots and leeks,
He had thrown in the pot.
He gave a brief stare,
But the thumb wasn't there –
His wife said, "It must be!"
The cook said, "It's not!"
Said his wife, "That's a worry!
We really must hurry,

For this is a serious matter,
Your thumb's in the food,
And it must be pursued –
Search every plate and each platter!"

The cook shed a tear,
He said "It's not here!
The Queen is still waiting –
Oh, what an ordeal!"
He gulped down with dread,
"She will chop of my head –
I cannot be late,
When I'm serving her meal"
Said his wife then, "Be quick –
For it makes me quite sick –
To think of myself all alone –
You earn all the money,
It makes me go funny –
To think of myself on my own!"

So, the cook (as agreed)
Served the Queen with great speed,
At her usual time,
He set forth her soup.
She sipped from her spoon,
And was over the moon –
She cried, "My good man –
You have pulled quite a coup!
This soup is superb,
You can taste every herb,
And the meat is like nothing before,
It's super; it's bliss,

But please tell me this,
Do you think that I might have some more?"

The cook gave a cry,
"You can't! This is why:
The soup that I made you,
Should not have had meat!
My thumb's gone astray..."
He called out in dismay,
"Look at my hand!
It is left incomplete!"
"How strangely obscene,"
Cried Her Highness, the Queen,
"Your head should be chopped right away,
But strangely enough,
I enjoyed all the stuff,
That you served me at teatime today!"

She stared at the cook –
"You are off of the hook,
I'm not always mean,
As I hope that you know!
Return to your job,
Put the pot on the hob,
Bring me more soup,
And be quick as you go!
Be sure not to linger,
I want to have finger,
Then we will see how it goes –
When your fingers have gone,
I will gladly move on,
To a soup that is made from your toes!"

The Hibernation Poem

I wish that I could hibernate,
When life becomes a hustle,
And anywhere that's out of doors,
Is quite the squally bustle,
Oh, to be a hedgehog,
What a splendid, blissful thing!
I'd leave behind the winter,
And I'd see you in the spring!

No news at all would penetrate,
My cosy, comfy hide,
I'd be nestled in my silken leaves,
And safe from what's outside,
Deep underground in happy dreams,
I'd pass the restful hours,
Till the doom and gloom has gone away,
And sunshine brings the flowers.

The Frog who Loved Herself

A frog on a log, in the month known as August,
Looked down in a pool and believed herself gorgeous.

A toad hopping by, saw the frog on the log,
In the month known as August,
He watched like a fool, as she gazed in the pool,
Believing herself to be gorgeous.

"Greetings and hi," said the toad hopping by,
To the frog on the log, in the month known as August,
But no answer came as it started to rain,
And the night had grown cool, as she stared in the pool,
Believing herself to be gorgeous.

The toad gave a sigh for he'd had no reply,
To his greeting of 'Hi', that he'd said hopping by,
To the frog on the log, in the month known as August.
Her thoughts were elsewhere, she did not see him there,
Just fixed on the pool, like to watch was a rule,
And believing herself to be gorgeous.

The moon shining bright on a late summer's night,
The toad gave a sigh for still no reply,
To his greeting of 'Hi' that he'd said hopping by,
To the frog on the log, in the month known as August.

He watched her intently, he loved her immensely,
And thought her not cruel – she was lost in the pool,
Believing herself to be gorgeous.

A fox saw the toad as he stalked down the road,
With the moon shining bright on a late summer's night,
That was filled with a sigh, for still no reply,
To the greeting of 'Hi' that was spoke hopping by,
To the frog on the log, in the month known as August.
The toad sat a-drooling, his fervour not cooling,
He heard not the mewl of the scarlet-clad ghoul,
Who advanced on the pool,
And the frog who believed herself gorgeous.

Yes, the fox saw the toad as he stalked down the road,
With the moon gleaming bright on a late summer's night,
He gave not a pause, as he snapped with his jaws,
And the moon wept a tear as she shone.
Then left quite alone, was the frog, on her own,
Though she knew not who'd been or who'd gone.

By the pool sat the frog, in the month known as August,
She sat there agog and believed herself gorgeous.

In the fox was the toad, lamenting to Cupid,
"How sorry am I?" And he thought himself stupid.

MELODIOUS
SERENDIPITY

The Word Snatcher

He'd gather the words from out of their mouths,
Of the people who lived by the stream,
He'd wrap them in silk and then hang them on clouds,
Where they'd sparkle in sun like a dream,
And he'd watch with a smile as the folks down below,
Looked hard in their quests to recall,
A word from their minds that they felt they should know,
But now couldn't grasp them at all.

High in the heavens, and out of their sight,
Letters hung like baubles on trees,
They glimmered at dawn and they glinted at night,
And they chimed with the touch of the breeze,
Yet down in the town, their faces were blank,
For the words they now struggled to place,
If only they knew, t'was a thief they should thank,
For the puzzling look on each face.

In truth, I should say, he knew not of his wrong,
Till one morning, he heard a sad cry,
A child who'd misplaced the words of a song,
From a time that had long travelled by.
A gift from his mom; the most sweetest of things,
Before she had gone to her rest,
More precious than gems or one hundred gold rings,
A lullaby simple and blessed.

And the snatcher of words felt the pain in his soul,
Like rivers through caves running deep,
And the glow in his heart was blackened like coal,
No refuge was found in his sleep.
And so, he resolved to return what he'd taken,
He sprinkled the words from above,
So, the people below would arise and awaken,
To gifts full of wonder and love.

And what a delight in the glow of the dawn,
To have music and words once again,
How speeches and hope filled the arms of the morn,
From the women and children and men.
And the snatcher of words felt contentment and joy,
As he listened to each cherished tune,
His favourite of all: from a mom to her boy,
Lit his eyes like the light of the moon.

At the Fairground

Toffee apples, teddy bears,
Take a teacup ride,
Steeplechase,
Haunted house,
With frightened screams inside.

Roundabouts and carousels,
(A spinning sort of cousin)
Bouncy castle, hook-a-duck,
With dodgems at the dozen.

Ferris wheels and ghost trains,
With spectres in the sky!
Helter skelter, coconuts,
Hit them off the shy.

Burgers, hot dogs, candyfloss,
Goldfish in a bowl,
Fortune tellers read your cards,
And gaze within your soul.

Popcorn, hoopla, waltzers,
And laugher all the while,
Enter for two shillings,
And leave with a quite a smile.

Fishing by Twilight

Perched upon the jetty, beneath the inky, twilight sky,
Reflections in the water as the moon and stars pass by,
All the world is quiet, save the reeds that catch the gentle breeze,
And the stifled breath of nervous hope,
That punctuates times such as these.

Our pond seemed like an ocean, which spread beyond our line of sight,
Carried all our hopes and dreams on journeys through the coming night,
And in that blissful silence, we said a prayer, we made a wish,
That by luck or chance or magic,
We would break our duck and catch a fish.

Hypnotic were the ripples, they danced before our sleepy gaze,
Till suddenly, commotion! The waters part a thousand ways!
And on the line, there's tension! A hard-fought clash of strength and wit,
Hearts anticipating; what, beneath is waiting?
And who will be the victor out of tiny us and it?

"Got one!" came my best friend's cry, and there, inside her lap,
The minnow lay quite dazed and stunned as if within some peaceful nap,
And I guess I feel half envious, half proud of what I see,
I smile congratulations, but I really hope that next time,
She'll look that way at me.

Haiku of the Elements

Quencher of my thirst,
Tranquil sleeps or filled with rage,
Roams free, ever flows.

Bringer of my breath,
Apple blossom, autumn leaf,
Carried in your hands.

Bearer of my weight,
Fertile meadow, caverns deep,
Mother of the trees.

Stoker of my soul,
Burning with a vibrant flame,
Endless spark that shines.

The House by the Sea

Of the numerous places,
I know I could be,
I am glad I am here,
In my house by the sea.

Where,
From out of the window,
I gaze upon waves,
That once carried the ships,
To the smugglers' caves,
Or the fleet to their battles,
Or the merchants to deals,
Or pirates to plunder,
And greater ordeals.

But now there are dinghies,
At innocent leisure,
Though I still espy hunters,
Marauding for treasure,
In rock pools they scramble,
Through sand dunes they roam,
Exploring for trinkets,
Brought in on the foam.

And then to the dusk,
At the end of the day,
Where the fishermen wait,
And the sand hoppers play,
And I am at peace,
So all at once pledge,
That I'm grateful I'm here,
Looking out from my ledge.

For of all of the places,
I know I could be,
Nowhere else warms,
Like my house by the sea.

Message in a Bottle

Always choose kind,
And calmness of mind,
Show warmth with the glow of your eyes,
Appreciate words,
And listen to birds,
And cherish the bluest of skies.

Imagine and dream,
By the sea or a stream,
Keep the wonder of youth by your side,
Be captured by art,
Show the glow of your heart,
Be a teacher, a friend and a guide.

Make time for the stars,
Protect what is ours,
For the world is a gift to keep safe,
Journey prepared,
As a road should be shared,
And a footstep be taken with faith.

Be gracious with trust,
If it breaks, then you must,
Find another who'll take better care,
Offer your hand,
Take a walk on the sand,
And savour the freshness of air.

Sit amongst flowers,
Pass away hours,
Taking no heed of the time,
Go looking for reasons,
To savour the seasons,
And chance to get lost in a rhyme.

Learn from the trees,
And the song of the breeze,
For in nature, comes freedom and wealth,
Every once and a while,
Find a mirror and smile,
And be gentle and good to yourself.

About the Author

Christopher Powell was born in 1982 and works in the primary education sector in Sandwell in the West Midlands. On reading, *A Child's Garden of Verse* by Robert Louis Stevenson, he became hooked on the power of poems and went on to add Lewis Carroll, Roald Dahl and A.A. Milne to his list of literary inspirations. He is thankful for books and for language, and the wonderful power they possess. He counts a happy childhood as one of his greatest gifts and hopes just a small fragment of his work might inspire others like he himself has so often been inspired.